Beginner's Guide to Investing

How to Make Money in Stocks in 3 Easy Steps

Thembi Buthelezi

www.stock-market-for-beginners-school.com

Beginner's Guide to Investing

Printed in the United States of America

Stock Market For Beginners School Legal Notice

It should not be assumed that the *methods,* techniques and stock market basics courses taught by Stock Market For Beginners School will be profitable or that they will not result in losses. Past results are not necessarily indicative of future results. Stock Market For Beginners School Provides Educational Courses Intended For Better Stock Market Understanding. We are not a broker nor do we offer investing buy or sell recommendations. **NO REPRESENTATION IS BEING MADE THAT ANY ACCOUNT WILL OR IS LIKELY TO ACHIEVE PROFITS OR LOSSES SIMILAR TO THOSE SHOWN.**

www.stockmarketforbeginnersschool.com

THANK YOU FOR PURCHASING MY BOOK.

PLEASE **REVIEW** THIS BOOK ON AMAZON.

I need your feedback to make the next version better. Thank you so much!

Get The Audio Book FREE!

JUST TO SAY THANKS FOR PURCHASING MY BOOK, GO TO THE PAGE BELOW TO DOWNLOAD THE AUDIO VERSION **100% FREE!**

www.stock-market-for-beginners-school.com

Table of Contents

Part 1

Are you ready to change your Financial Future?

Are you frustrated with the conflicting information about stock trading and the stock market?

Does it worry you when you are at the "day job" and can't place a trade "at the proper time"?

How awful does it feel to purchase a stock "low" only to see it go lower!?

Are you unable to "pull the trigger" on a stock because you are not entirely confident?

Does the fear and uncertainty of losing a lot of money in the stock market prevent you from even starting to trade?

Do you feel overwhelmed and intimidated by the vast amounts of information and knowledge you need to learn so that you master trading the stock market?

Are you bewildered by technical analysis and balance sheets?

Does the thought of not knowing what your broker is doing with your money in the stock market make you have sleepless nights?

Welcome to Stock Market For Beginners School. A school dedicated to empower beginner stock market traders with proven, undiluted, step by step, surefire strategies to maximize their profits, build wealth and minimize their losses in the stock market.

YOU HAVE PICKED UP THE RIGHT STOCK MARKET TRADING BOOK, SPECIFICALLY WRITTEN FOR MY FRIENDS JUST STARTING OUT IN TRADING THE MARKET.

Soon your stock market questions will be answered and all your stock market troubles will be soothed away. Since graduating business school, I have passionately studied, analyzed and traded the market. It is now your turn to learn the stock market, pick the right stocks, know when the stock market is going to go up and know when to sell your stocks before the another major market meltdown? I am dedicated to make the stock market a fun and easy concept for friends like you.

I started trading the financial markets after leaving business school over 15 years ago. I had my first taste of the trading lifestyle at the age of 21. I was a successful Forex trader making an obnoxious amount of money. This lifestyle gave me the freedom to do whatever I wanted to do, whenever I want to do it.

At the age of 24, I managed to completely destroy my trading account with 7 trades. Mind you, this was no small account. In just 3 years, I had built up my trading account from $5000.00 to a rather healthy trading account where I could trade standard lots, a Forex trading term for big position size used by institutional investors like HSBC. In other words a lot is a "lot" of money. And now it was all gone. For the first time in years I had to get a job so I could save up some money to start trading again. I had never had to have a 9-5 job after I learned how to trade at the age of 21.

As I look back on it, blowing up my trading account and losing all my "easy money" was the most humbling thing that could've happened to me. I am so grateful that the lesson came earlier in life rather than later.

This experience taught me to respect the market; it forced me to create trading rules and taught me how to treat trading like a small business. Without working capital you are done. Your trading business will shut down until you can fund it again.

After spending a year working at non fun jobs, I applied and got a position working for an equities trading firm in New York City. This is where my love affair with the stock market began. I finally became a professional trader and not just a gifted Forex rookie. I learned the insider secrets that Wall Street professionals don't want the general public to know and I mastered the art and science of online stock trading.

IN THIS BOOK I'M GOING TO SHARE THE SECRETS THAT WALL STREET DOESN'T WANT YOU TO KNOW. I'M GOING TO REVEAL:

Why beginner traders inevitably purchase trades that are going down without knowing it

How to gain the confidence in your newfound skills to place a trade without hesitation from fear of loss.

How to perform technical analysis like the Wall Street professionals.

How to learn and grow the absolutely necessary skills to identify profitable trades in any market and earn up to 50% profits even in bearish markets.

I was once a beginner...

"From the bottom of my heart I would like to thank you for the education you have given me on trading in the stock market."

I was completely lost in the market until you were nice enough to take me in as one of your students. I learned much more about the stock market than I ever thought possible from your classes. And by doing so, my

passion and enthusiasm has grown week by week, as you taught me the ways to trade the market.

Before, I would get emails from so called gurus on what to trade and what not to trade. Friends would sometimes tell me; oh this is the stock you should trade. And where did that get me?

Nowhere!!! I would win a trade here, lose a trade there, but never get ahead. Then you came along, and gave me an analogy in the stock market about hogs, sheep, ostriches, and professionals.

During your classes I started to feel more and more like a professional. And what gave me that confidence was your education on technical analysis. Where would I be today without technical analysis? Back with the gurus, and friends giving me advice like hogs and sheep.

I am not saying technical analysis is the only thing I learned from Trading School, but it was one of the most important things that has helped me to become more successful and passionate about trading."

Your Student and now close friend,

Bob Zientek

"I have come to have a better understanding of the market, I am capable of becoming a successful trader."

Just three months ago, I was looking for ways to enter the market and thus generate more income. So while searching the internet I found Stock Market For Beginners School. The word that caught my attention was "BEGINNER". You will hardly find someone below my beginner level, so I thought "This is what I am looking for". I religiously listened and digested every single introductory video lesson I was sent, and little by little I realized that reading the charts and analyzing the market was not like trying to understand Chinese anymore.

I have learned the way the market moves and how to approach and take advantage of those moves. Certainly with more experience will come better moves and in time more profits. In essence the possibilities are limitless once I become a consistently profitable trader.

Now I am much more confident about approaching the market. I am aware that there will be ups and downs, but the downs have to be controlled.

If you are a beginner like I was all I can tell you is that if you decide to join Stock Market For Beginners School you are making the right choice.

Wilmer

THIS BOOK IS ONLY FOR SERIOUS BEGINNER STOCK MARKET TRADERS WHO WANT TO MAKE A LOT OF MONEY IN THE NEXT 2-5 MONTHS IN THE STOCK MARKET

If you are serious about learning how to trade the stock market successfully and are willing to put in the work and time it takes to master it, I want you to carry on reading this book to the end.

This will be the only book that gives you proven step by step strategies that work in any market condition. This will be your stock market guide that you can refer back to when you need expert guidance. I promise to give you easy to understand content, and powerful actionable steps to guide you through the stock market maze, so you can be one of those successful traders who lives their dreams and makes an obscene amount of money, easily and effortlessly.

Could This Be Just Another "All Hype, No Real Results Kindle Book"?

Now, I know some of you are skeptical. I'm sure you're thinking, "the stock market is a casino, trading the stock market is like gambling, there are no rules, I'm going to lose my shirt, my pants, my house, my marriage and all my money". I can assure you that there are no absolutes in the stock market. I can also assure you that you are going to lose money 20-30% of the time, but what if I can teach you how to make serious money 70% of the time and lose very little 30% of the time.

All professional traders lose money, yes. Even the guy that looks after your 401k and IRA. It's the cost of doing business as a trader. Astute traders lose small and ALWAYS WIN BIG. I can teach you how to make money without risking too much.

Don't Wait Any LONGER; You Might Miss The Next Bull Market!

If you have missed the 2009-2013 bull market because you had been afraid to enter the stock market, today IS THE DAY you put your financial future in your OWN hands. Today is the day you learn how to invest like a professional and start living the life of your dreams. I laid out the steps in the following chapter for you to follow, so turn to the next page now. Don't wait, you'll miss out on the next bull market, or even worse... You might be caught buying long into the coming stock market selloff.

Chapter 1

3 Steps to Build Stock Market Wealth

Over the past 4 years I have been actively engaged in developing beginner traders to become astute professionals in the stock market. The first year I wrote articles and created many videos for my website, Stock Market For Beginners School. In the second year I started taking on private coaching students. I knew that I had found my calling in life. After every single coaching call I would get off the phone and feel elated that I spurred a big shift in perception for another wonderful person. I was, and am, always particularly excited to help beginner traders master the stock market.

During this first year of coaching my team of students, I learned a tremendous amount of valuable information about beginner traders and how they approach the stock market. Not only do they approach trading in a haphazard manner, but they also made trading decisions based largely from a place of fear. As I intently listened to my students as they shared their experiences about the stock market, I realized that many of us have been taught to fear the stock market and leave investing to the experts.

We have never been empowered to make our own financial decisions. The old financial planning slogan is: "You do what you do best, we'll do what we do best, look after your money".

This approach to building wealth and financial security might have worked in the 50s but I'm not sure it works so well in the 21st century. As the cost of living increases, as inflation rises and as more and more people find themselves struggling in their retirement years, I wonder how the experts think they can keep selling a dream that is no longer viable.

My friend, I'm not a financial planner, and I have no desire to be one. I enjoy trading my own money in the stock market and knowing that I am the only one responsible for my financial future. I have nothing against financial planners and stock market gurus who tell people what stocks to buy on late night TV, but I'm just a girl who wants to help 1 million people learn how the stock market really works so that they create financial freedom for themselves and their families.

Sometimes I'm much too much a dreamer. I believe that if everyone made enough money to live happy , adventurous and prosperous lives, there would be less poverty, less crime, less angry, depressed and miserable people in this world. Maybe I wear my heart on my sleeve and believe in magic, but I believe we can all make money in the stock market and there will still be plenty left over.

FEAR OR GREED?

For as long as the market existed, fear and greed have ruled the financial markets. Either we are taught to fear losing all our money, or we are encouraged to invest and make more money than our little hearts know what to do with. How do we strike the balance?

Recently, I was in sunny Orlando, Florida, a haven for the comfortably retired. I was having lunch with my sister at a restaurant when the lovely folks sitting at a table next to us, engaged us in conversation. So we both obliged and found out that these lovely 69 year olds were miserably retired and hugely in debt. The only joy in their lives was the sunshine in Florida.

I was perplexed. I couldn't understand how this beautiful couple, who had worked all their lives, had once had it all and lived in a 4000sqf house in Ohio, could retire in Florida, heavily in debt, only relying on social security.

My heart broke for them, because I could tell that they were just a nice and hardworking couple who had entrusted their financial future to someone else. I didn't want to dig further into their financial situation, because I sensed it was a sensitive subject for them, but I knew in that moment that more people needed to learn how to handle their own money so they could retire debt free.

Even if you have 30 years until your retirement, I encourage you to learn the steps in this book; I encourage you to implement what you learn so you can secure your financial future. We can no longer just rely on financial advisors and stock market gurus to give us advice about our money and how to invest it. We, as a global community, need to take responsibility for our own financial future.

THE 3 STEPS TO BUILD WEALTH IN THE STOCK MARKET.

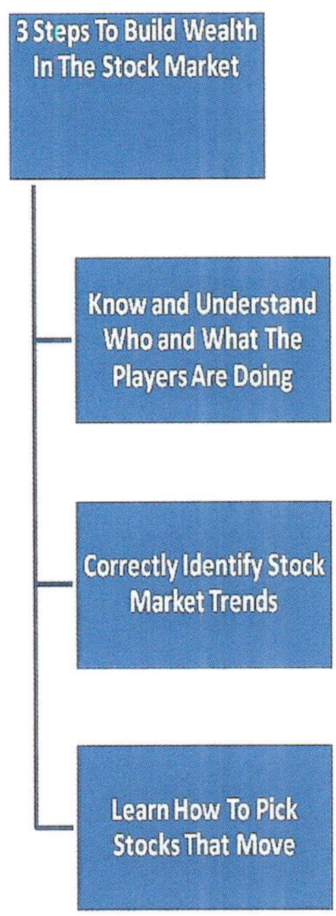

The flow chart above walks you through the building blocks to stock market wealth. Without these three steps or building blocks, it will be hard to consistently make money in the stock market year after year. You'll be stuck looking for the next broker who promises that they can help you make bigger returns, the next money manager who promises that they can beat the S&P or you'll just keep chasing the elusive *holy grail of trading*: "a sure thing". I want to forewarn you; *the holy grail of trading*, does not exist. There are 3-12 main building blocks that every trader should learn. After that, it's up to you how you implement those building blocks. In this book, I'm going to start with the first 3 building blocks. In the next few books of this series we will explore the rest of the building blocks.

You can buy 30 different trading systems and they will all teach you the same building blocks. The challenge for beginner traders is in implementing the steps. That is where your friend Thembi comes into play. I will make the building blocks super easy, simple enough for a 10 year old to implement. This will save you time, money and reach trading nirvana quickly.

LET'S RECAP THE 3 STEPS TO BUILD STOCK MARKET WEALTH.

1. **Who are the stock market players?**

   Who are you competing against in the stock market?

   What do they know that you don't know?

   Are you sure you are on the right side of the trade?

2. **What are the 3 stock market trends?**

   When do you buy a stock?

When do you sell your stock?

When do you completely stay out of the stock market?

3. How to pick stocks that are on the brink of a big move?

Do penny stocks light the way to stock market riches?

What kind of stocks do wall street professionals trade?

SO, NOW THAT YOU KNOW THE THREE STEPS TO BUILD STOCK MARKET WEALTH, WHY SHOULD YOU CARE?

Trading or investing your own money should be treated like running a small business. Without the right accountant, your small business will eventually be subjected to IRS audits. Without sufficient capital your small business will not be able to grow. Without the right product (stocks, in our case) your small business will not be able to make money. Without the right pricing strategy, your business will lose money. Without the right location, you will not have enough customers.

So many novice traders don't see the importance of planning their trading strategies. So many beginner investors think trading is all about finding the right stock at the right time. They fail to implement all three of the steps to build stock market wealth. If you don't implement all 3 steps, you will lose money. Period. This I can guarantee you. You will lose a lot of money.

PART 2

THE THREE STEPS TO STOCK MARKET WEALTH EXPLAINED

CHAPTER 2

ARE YOU A HOG, SHEEP OR PROFESSIONAL?

The stock market is a combination of hogs, sheep and professionals. Let's talk about the New York Stock Exchange. The New York Stock Exchange is in downtown New York, right? We all know that. It is a building and it is filled with people buying and selling stocks all day long. Beginner traders think that investing is about buying and selling stocks or shares. This is partly true, but not entirely true. From a professional trader's point of view, trading is the art of whose opinion is right and whose opinion is wrong. It's that simple. I know this nugget of knowledge sounds incredibly vague, but before I lose you, let me explain...

When you decide to buy a stock are you really trading the building on Wall Street? Are you really buying a stock in a company or are you trading the opinions of hogs, sheep and professionals about the stock that you are buying? If you think of the stock market not as an environment or a specific place, but rather as people's opinions about the stocks that you want to invest in, only then will your understanding of the stock market become completely different.

There are only three participants that make up the stock market. Hogs, sheep and professionals.

Novice traders think the stock market is a combination of companies and the stocks. Companies and stocks cannot buy and sell themselves. Human beings, meaning you and I can buy and sell stocks. Therefore, when you engage in trading or investing, you are actually buying and selling the opinions of other investors about the particular stock you are trading.

During the three steps, I'm going to show you, why it's not a stock or company that you're trading. In truth, you are actually trading people's opinions about the stock. I'm going to prove it to you over and over and over again. By the end of the three steps you'll be able to tell what other investors' opinions are about any stock you want to buy.

LET ME FORMALLY INTRODUCE THE STOCK MARKET PLAYERS

Again, the stock market is comprised of hogs, sheep and professionals. Let's first spot the hogs in the stock market.

Hogs are uneducated retail traders working from their computers at home. There you go I said it. I'm sorry if I hurt your feelings but this truth has to be stated. In my years of trading I have met numerous hogs. Here is what is interesting about hogs:

Hogs take 1, 2 or 3 day seminars in a stuffy room, filled with other hogs and an instructor who is boring as Ben Stein but not nearly as smart and successful. I've taken those seminars, and by the end of day 2, I have lost 90% of the content that the instructor taught in day one.

After the hogs take these seminars, they think they are trading rock stars. They think they have the ultimate trading *holy grail* and they are off to the races. They don't demo trade (trade paper money) while they test their new strategy; they immediately put in real money and in a span of 6 months, they have lost it all.

When they lose all their money, they blame everyone. They blame the broker, they blame the stupid trading platform, they blame the boring instructor and they carry on blaming someone or something. Hogs never take any responsibility for losing their money.

Because hogs never accept responsibility, they are doomed to repeat the vicious cycle. They find another trading course online, buy it, implement the new trading strategy, and they lose money once again. Then the blame cycle starts all over again.

By the 3rd seminar or online trading course, ashamed to tell their spouse how much money they have lost, Hogs decide that the stock market is rigged and they will tell anyone and everyone who crosses their path.

This is very sad. I have heard a lot of horror stories about how hard-working, honest and really lovely people lose all of their money in the stock market. I absolutely feel for people who have lost their money in the stock market, if you are one of those people, **please understand that I am writing this book to save you from another stock market disaster episode.**

I'm writing this book to help you awaken to the secrets that Wall Street doesn't want you to know. It's not your fault that you didn't know how Wall Street really works. You were doing the best you could with the knowledge that you had. Now that you know better, I hope that you are going to do better.

WHY THE 2 OR 3 DAY STOCK MARKET TRADING SEMINAR MODEL DOESN'T WORK.

The human brain filters out 80-90% of the content it receives all day long. Yes, you might be eager to learn how to trade the stock market. You might have paid a lot of money to learn how to trade, but by the end of day 3, you have forgotten 80% of what you learned. So you see, if you've been a hog in the stock market, it's really not your fault that you lost money. You forgot most of what you learned during the seminars that you attended.

The only way I have found to really master the stock market is by consuming small chunks of content on a weekly basis. I know, I know, you want to learn this content quickly so you can make your millions. But truth be told, there is no one who can learn to trade the stock market by reading a book or attending a 3 day seminar. You actually have to practice what you learn every week in a demo trading account.

Enough about the hogs. They are lovely people, but most of the time they are misinformed about what it really takes to trade the stock market.

Do you know a sheep?

Sheep are those investors who come home and religiously watch CNBC. Don't get me wrong, there is absolutely nothing inherently "wrong" with Fast Money or Mr. Cramer. In fact they are quite entertaining. The problem with sheep is that they call into these stock market shows on CNBC and beg for stock market advice. Sheep want to be lead, they want to be told what stocks to buy, when to buy it and then when the stock tips don't work they also play the blame game.

Unlike the Hogs, the Sheep just want to be led. At least Hogs make an effort to educate themselves about the stock market. Sheep want surefire stock tips. Most of the time Sheep want these surefire stock tips for FREE.

Now there is an interesting word, FREE. Nothing is ever free. My mentor used to say, Thembi, in the stock market there is no FREE lunch. Even if it's a stock market guru giving you FREE advice on what stocks to buy, there is always a catch.

The zero sum game explained

Before you dismiss my FREE lunch statement and hate me for telling my version of the truth (playing the blame game), let me explain that the stock market zero sum game.

The stock market zero sum game states that for every buyer there is a seller. You cannot buy a stock and not have someone sell you the stock that you want to buy. If you call your broker and ask them to buy ABCD stock for you, they have to place a buy order and someone who already owns that stock has to be willing to sell you the stock that you want to buy.

If you want to sell a stock, someone has to be willing to buy the stock from you. There are always an equal number of buyers and sellers in the stock market.

The million dollar question is, what does the person willing to sell you the stock that you want to buy know that you don't know? Why are they willing to sell you that stock?

Let's assume that you think ABCD stock is cheap and a good buy at $40. You open up your Scott Trade account and place a buy order at $40.50. Great, you're elated and can't wait to make your millions in that stock.

The Million Dollar Question is: What information does this buyer/seller have that you don't? If you got the stock tip from a stock market guru on TV, what information do they have about the stock that they are not telling you? Stock market gurus are professionals, they are not in the business of giving away free stock tips. They are in the business of entertaining you on TV. It's a **fallacy** that they want to help you make money in the stock market; they are looking out for their profits not yours.

THE PROFESSIONAL STOCK MARKET TRADER

Professional traders know more than you about what is happening in the stock market. They have dedicated their professional lives and careers to understanding the stock market.

Their bread and butter come from trading the stock market. These individuals may have a team of researchers and that help them gain access to information that you will never have. How can independent traders like you (and me at one time) possibly compete with the professionals? Well, professional traders come in all shapes and sizes.

There are Institutional traders, those who trade for banks, investment banking firms and brokerage firms.

There are independent professional traders, who trade from home and trade their own money.

There are hedge fund traders, who trade money for very wealthy individuals.

Hogs and sheep compete against these traders on a daily basis when they attempt to trade the stock market. Hogs and sheep cannot win because professional traders make it their business to know as much as possible about the stocks they are trading. Professional traders tend to know a lot about the stock market.

As I'm writing this paragraph, I can hear you saying to yourself, "why bother? I don't have the time to learn everything there is to know about the stock market. I have a full time job, a spouse, children, 2 pets and a mortgage. Who has the time? I may as well put my head in the sand and hope that I have enough money to retire!"

Have a little faith. I'm writing this book so I can help you learn how to think and trade like a professional trader. My intention is that everyone who reads this book will aspire to think and trade like an independent professional trader, instead of trading like a hog or sheep.

Hogs and sheep always end up in the slaughter house. Professionals may lose money, but in the long run they end up ahead of the hogs and sheep.

Now that you know who the three stock market players are and how they behave in the stock market, I would like to help you identify the professionals at play in the stock market. Please pay close attention, your job is going to be spotting the professionals in the stock market. Once you do, you'll want to trade in the same direction that they are trading. You don't want to be buying when the professionals are selling, you don't want to be selling when the professionals are buying. You want to mimic the behavior of the professionals on Wall Street. This is how to make money as a beginner trader.

CHAPTER 3

YOU WILL END UP DEAD (BROKE) IF YOU DISOBEY THE TREND

In chapter 2, we learnt who the players are and we discussed a little bit about the market. You now have a little bit of market understanding. Now we're going to go a little deeper into our market understanding so we can really understand the market whether we're in a bearish or a bullish environment. We'll talk a little bit about the players in the bearish and the bullish environment. Okay?

Are we bullish or are we bearish? How do you know what the trend is in a stock or in the stock market as a whole? Here's a question: Would you buy a stock that is going to zero or would you sell a stock that is going higher? Now I'm sure you're thinking, "Oh my god, Thembi, this is such a dumb question! Why would you even ask such a stupid question?" But I've seen beginner investors and traders do this on a daily, weekly, monthly basis. I used to do that; I would be out selling stocks in a bullish environment and buying stocks in a bearish environment.

If you're buying a stock in a bearish environment, that stock can go to zero. We do this. The reason why we sell our stocks prematurely in a bullish environment is because we don't know how to recognize a bullish trend. The reason why we buy stocks that are falling is because we don't know how to recognize a bearish trend.

If I showed you a simple four step formula for recognizing whether the stock is in a bullish trend or a bearish trend, would you buy a stock in the bearish trend? Of course you wouldn't. **I'm going to give you that formula**

in this chapter. You have to carry on reading so you can get the formula. It's so easy, just four steps. Once you can correctly spot a trend, you will make more money than you know what to do with in the stock market. Let's talk about the trends.

In the stock market there are only three trends: there's a sideways trend where your stocks are just consolidating and are not doing anything. They're not going higher; they're not going any lower. They're just taking a break.

NEM Newmont Mining Corp. NYSE
© StockCharts.com
Open 32.15 High 34.25 Low 30.30 Close 32.28 Volume 110.8M Chg -0.12 (-0.37%)
NEM (Monthly) 32.28
MA(200) 35.72
Volume 110,840,384
70
65
60
55
50
45
40
35.72
32.28
30
25
11084
20
300M
200M
100M
A J O 07 A J O 08 A J O 09 A J O 10 A J O 11 A J O 12 A J O 13 A

As you can see in the stock above, this stock has been going sideways for 5 straight years. The stock price goes up to $60 and then the price comes down. The stock has a tough time moving higher than the $60 level.

Traders who trade stocks that are in a sideways pattern never really make any significant money. The stock goes up a little and then the stock comes crashing down. Hogs and sheep are the kind of traders that you would find in stocks like these. Professionals would never trade stocks that are in a sideways pattern. Instead professional traders prefer to only trade stocks that have a chart like this.

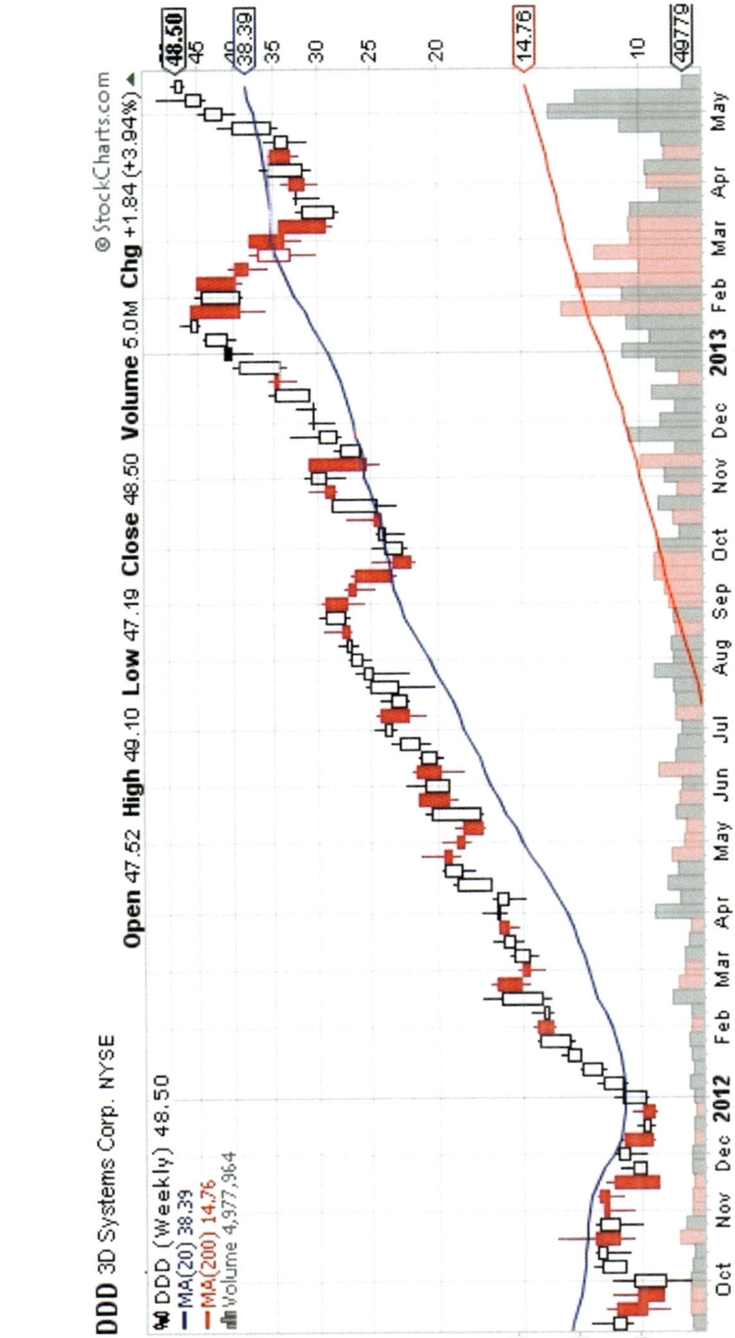
DDD 3D Systems Corp. NYSE
Open 47.52 High 49.10 Low 47.19 Close 48.50 Volume 5.0M Chg +1.84 (+3.94%)
© StockCharts.com
DDD (Weekly) 48.50
MA(20) 38.39
MA(200) 14.76
Volume 4,977,964

As you can see in the above chart, DDD has consistently made higher highs and its price has continued to go up and up since the beginning of 2012. These are the kind of stock that you want to find. These are the kinds of stocks that are going to make you rich in the stock market. Stay away from stocks that have a sideways trend.

HOW TO SPOT A TREND

If the stock market or stocks can either go up, down or sideways; how do you tell what trend it's in? Here's my little four steps formula. It's so easy it's ridiculous. If you knew how to do this you would have never lost money in the market, or if you learn how to do this you'll never lose a lot of money in the market.

But that's not true. That's so not true. In trading there is some risk and sometimes you will lose money. But if you lose money in a professional way, you will not be completely wiped out. Traders like the Hogs and the Sheep who just blindly buy are the ones who lose money and get wiped out in the market.

LET'S LOOK AT THE FOUR STEP FORMULA.

1. Yahoo.finance.com

2. Type the symbol of the stock you are researching

3. Select 3 month chart

3. Add the 200 day moving average

The first step is to go to Yahoo Finance. Everybody knows Yahoo Finance. You just type in Yahoo and you look at the finance section of yahoo. Then you type in the symbol of the stock that you're researching. If you're researching Apple you would type in AAPL. If you're researching General

Motors you would type in GM. Then click on the three months chart. You want to get a three-month view of the stock.

Here is another important aspect of looking at a chart on Yahoo. You want to make sure that you look at a chart with candles instead of a line or bar chart. Candles give you more information about what the professionals are committed to do in the stock. If the stock that you are looking at has huge green candles, and the trend is above the 200 day MA, you can rest assured that the trend is strongly bullish. Look at the example of the SPY in December of 2012 and June of 2012.

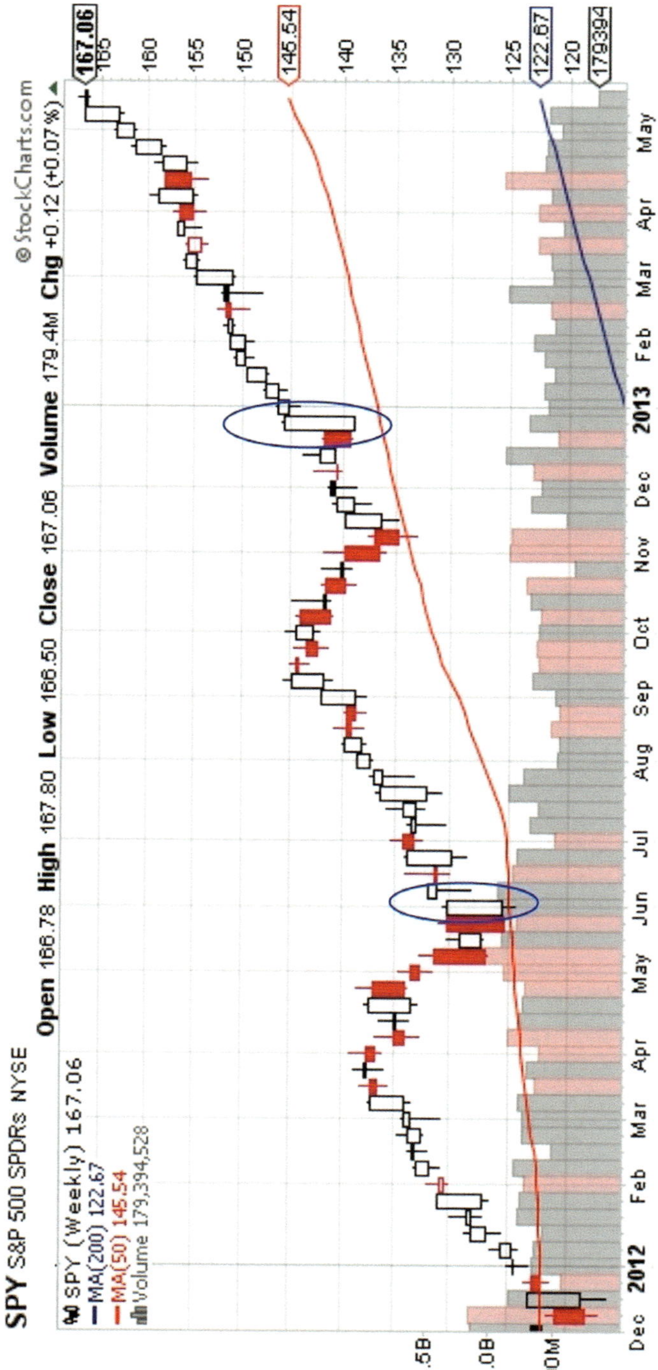
SPY S&P 500 SPDRs NYSE
Open 166.78 High 167.80 Low 166.50 Close 167.06 Volume 179.4M Chg +0.12 (+0.07%)
© StockCharts.com
SPY (Weekly) 167.06
MA(200) 122.67
MA(50) 145.54
Volume 179,394,528
167.06
145.54
122.67
179394
1.5B
1.0B
500M
Dec 2012 Feb Mar Apr May Jun Jul Aug Sep Oct Nov Dec 2013 Feb Mar Apr May

As soon as the price of the SPY touched the moving average, there was a huge green bar at an area of support and that huge green bar started the move higher.

In December 2012, we see another huge green bar that happens at an area of support which would be our moving average, and as you can see, that huge green bar started the bull trend that we are experiencing today. The SPY has been reaching new highs on a daily basis as a result of a huge inflow of money from professional traders and the US government. Traders who use line and bar charts don't get the valuable information that candles gives traders.

In the next book in this series, I will go deeper into Technical Analysis for Beginner Traders. I'm a technical analysis trader. I don't really rely on fundamental analysis much. If you are a fundamental analysis trader, I would advise you start learning how to read charts and start falling in love with technical analysis. WHY? LOOK at the chart of APPLE.

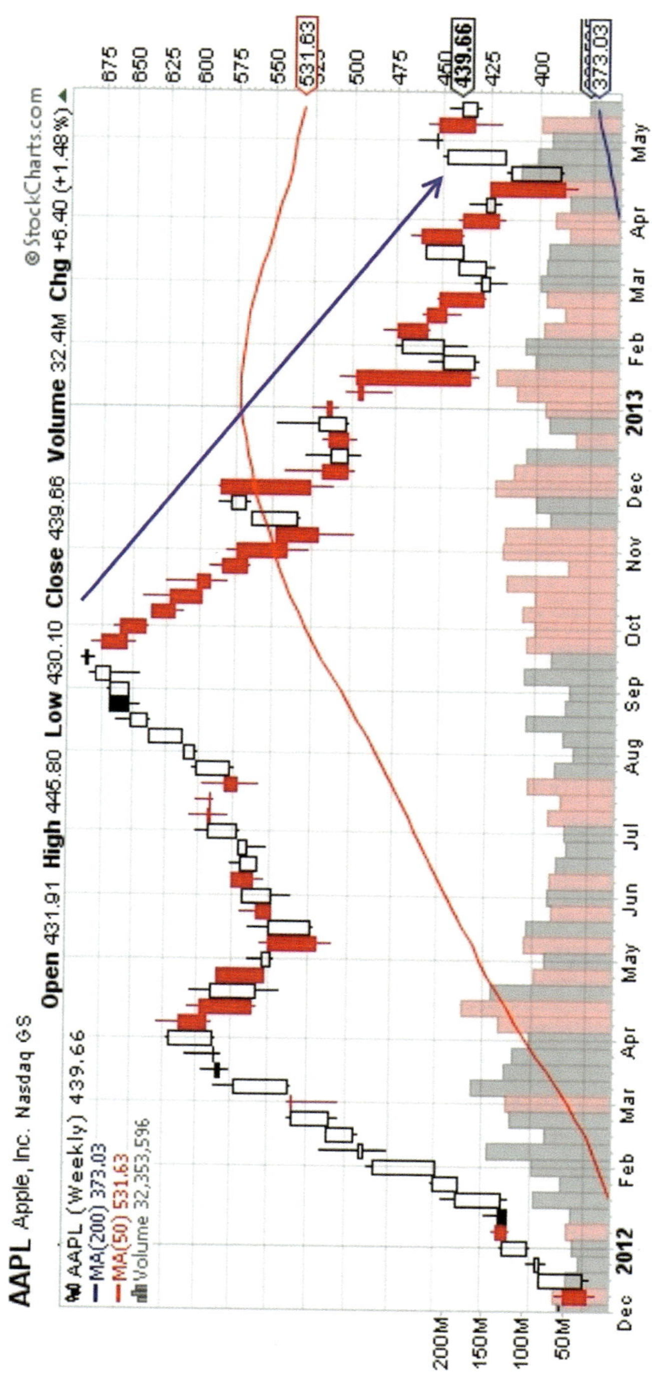

AAPL Apple, Inc. Nasdaq GS
Open 431.91 High 445.80 Low 430.10 Close 439.66 Volume 32.4M Chg +6.40 (+1.48%)
©StockCharts.com
AAPL (Weekly) 439.66
MA(200) 373.03
MA(50) 531.63
Volume 32,353,596

Apple has insane amounts of money in reserve, they produce amazing products (I'm an Apple lover), but the stock is falling apart. Why? Who knows? There are always rumors. Whether they are true or not, charts and candles never lie. If you're a fundamental trader, you'll be stuck holding the stock hoping that Apple will recover because of their business fundamentals. I might love Apple products, but I'll still short the stock, because professional traders are shorting the stock. Traders who follow the foot prints of professional traders make more money than traders who make up their own rules in the market.

Professional traders have more money than you and I will ever have, so the best way to make money is to just follow their direction in the market. If they are shorting a stock, short with them, and if they are buying a stock buy with them.

Big red and green candles in the market or on a stock chart represent professionals making their mark in that stock. If you can remember in the beginning of the book, I said we don't trade stocks or companies; we trade the opinions of hogs, sheep and professionals. Clearly the opinion of professionals (which is the opinion that counts) about APPLE right now is that the stock is weak. Thus, they are shorting it.

Oh my, I definitely went off topic. I started teaching you a lesson that I had intended to teach in the next book in this series. But that is ok; I want you to understand why candles are so important. Before you place your first trade, please make sure that you read my next book about how to understand technical analysis for beginner traders.

Now, let's get back to the 200 day moving average and Yahoo finance charts. Once you have typed in the symbol of the stock, then place a 200-day moving average on the chart... Voila: you will see exactly what trend that stock is. It's either in a sideways trend, in a bearish trend, or in a bullish trend. It is that easy.

Here's the secret. When the stock price is trading above the 200 day moving average, the stock can be said to be in a bullish trend. As you can see in the chart below, the price of the stock keeps going higher and higher.

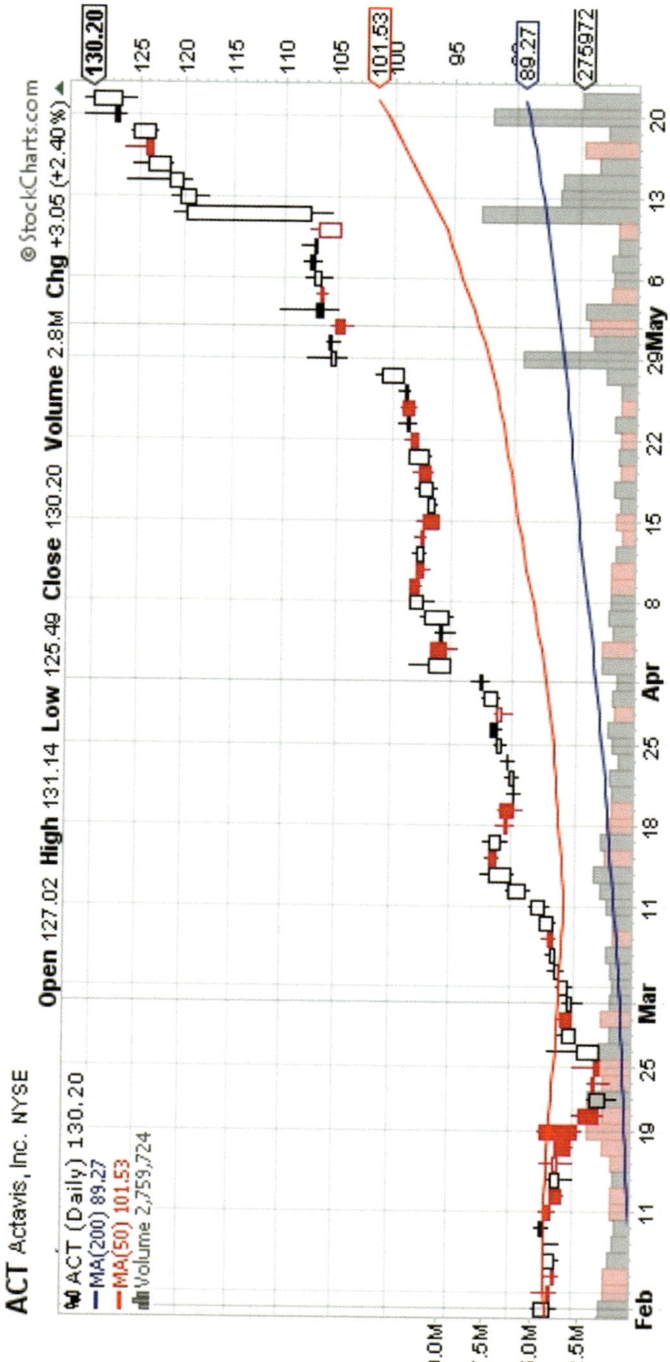

ACT Actavis, Inc. NYSE
©StockCharts.com
ACT (Daily) 130.20
MA(200) 89.27
MA(50) 101.53
Volume 2,759,724
Open 127.02 High 131.14 Low 125.49 Close 130.20 Volume 2.8M Chg +3.05 (+2.40%)
130.20
125
120
115
110
105
101.53
100
95
89.27
2759724
10.0M
7.5M
5.0M
2.5M
Feb
11
19
25
Mar
11
18
25
Apr
8
15
22
29
May
6
13
20

The price of Actavis has moved up from $89.27 to $130.20 in a span of 3 months. Once the stock bounced from the 200 day moving average in February 19th 2013, the stock price started climbing steadily until it reached $105.00. Now look at the big white bar, from $105.00 to $120.00 that happened on the 13th of May 2013. That bar was created by the professional traders with a lot of money to move that stock higher. If you're a beginner trader and you see a big bar like that in a stock chart, your opinion should be:

"WOW DUDE! The professionals know what they are doing to put in that much amount of money in that stock and move the price up that high. I should follow in the footsteps of professionals and buy the stock." Look at what happened as a result of that big white bar. The price of the stock continued going higher and higher. Now the stock is trading at $130.20 as of the writing of this book. Only professionals can create big bars like that within a particular stock or in the stock market as a whole.

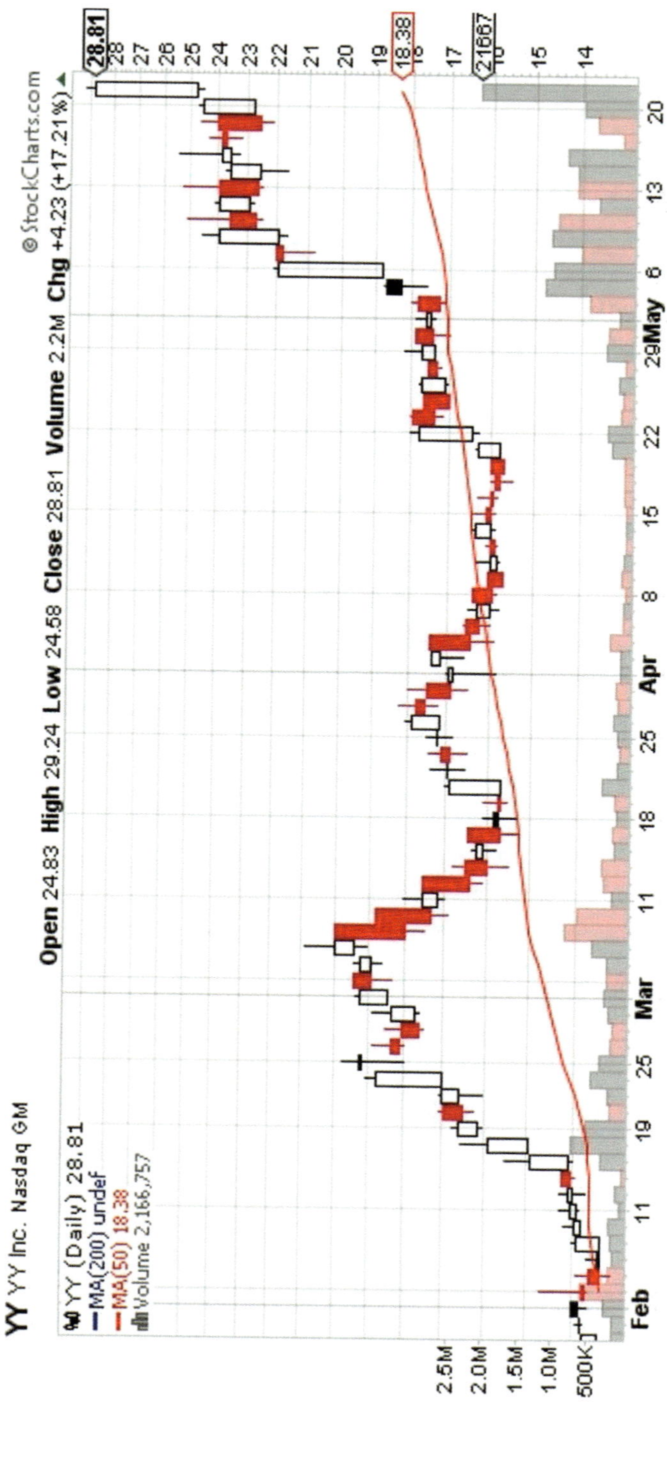

YY YY Inc. Nasdaq GM
YY (Daily) 28.81
MA(200) undef
MA(50) 18.38
Volume 2,166,757
Open 24.83 High 29.24 Low 24.58 Close 28.81 Volume 2.2M Chg +4.23 (+17.21%)
© StockCharts.com

Look at YY. The stock started trading above the 200 moving average in April 2013. Since then the stock price has moved up from $17 all the way up to $28.81. This is the power of buying stocks above the 200 day moving average!

Now let's take a look at stocks that are below the 200 day moving average. You will clearly see what will happen to YOU if you insist on buying stocks that are below the 200 day moving average. Not that long ago, people were going crazy about Gold and Silver. Look at what happens!

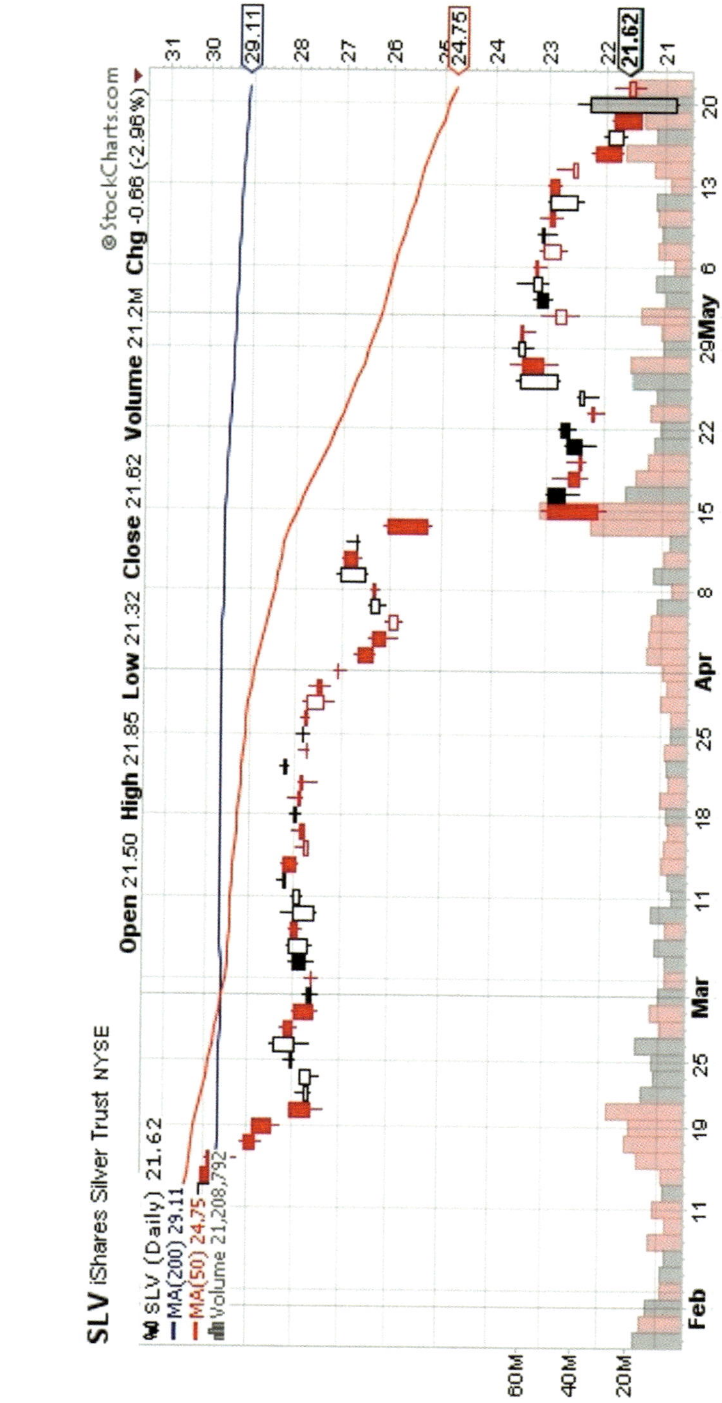
SLV iShares Silver Trust NYSE
@StockCharts.com
Open 21.50 High 21.85 Low 21.32 Close 21.62 Volume 21.2M Chg -0.66 (-2.96%)
SLV (Daily) 21.62
MA(200) 29.11
MA(50) 24.75
Volume 21,208,792
Feb
Mar
Apr
May
60M
40M
20M
29.11
24.75
21.62

The price of SLV keeps going lower and lower. The stock was trading at $29.11 in February and as of the writing of this book, the stock is now trading at $21.62. When stocks break the 200 day moving average they have a 60% probability of continuing the bearish trend. Do not buy stocks trading below the 200 day moving average. You will lose money!

A few months ago I started watching Wall Street Warriors. I found it on Hulu.com. It is a very entertaining show and if you haven't watched it, I suggest you go watch it. During one episode, stock brokers were calling up their "WHALE" clients and convincing them to buy stocks that were clearly under the 200 day moving average. One client (a sheep, I presume) bought so much stock from their broker, that I'm sure he lost over $200k. That investor didn't understand the 200 day moving average rule. If a stock is trading below the 200 day moving average, don't buy it, even if you love your broker and he has made money for you in the past!

If your broker calls you and says, "Hey John, I have an amazing stock pick for you, do you want to buy GLD, and it is very cheap right now? I think GLD is going to the moon." I want you to say to him, "Yeah, I don't think so. Thanks for the offer but you know what? Until GLD goes above the 200-day moving average, thanks. I'm not interested in buying GLD." If a stock is below the 200-day moving average, you don't know how low it can go. You, as a beginner trader should not be buying that stock.

The trend here is bearish. You should be shorting in a bearish environment. You should not be going long in a bearish environment. GLD is totally bearish. We don't know what's going to happen to GLD.

HOMEWORK TIME

I love, love, love homework. I always encourage my private coaching students to do their homework after every single lesson. Because when I give them homework they understand the lesson. Reading the lesson and thinking to yourself, "Yeah, yeah, yeah, that's so nice. Yup, I know about the 200-day moving average. Above bullish, below bearish." But until you actually go and do the homework yourself and you see it and you research 100 stocks and you see the exact picture for yourself, this lesson is never going to solidify. You want to create new neural pathways in your brain so that this education and this information will solidify in your brain.

Once you create neural pathways in your brain, you can just look at a stock and say, "Ah, yeah. I don't think so. I'm not buying that stock." You have to do the homework to master charts. You have to go do it yourself.

Now here's the homework. Take a look at stocks you own or stocks you may want to trade and ask yourself: is that stock in a bearish or a bullish trend? If you find that you keep buying stocks that are in a bearish trend, ask yourself, why are you buying those stocks? If your answer is, "I'm averaging down. I'm buying the stocks at a cheaper price," then I want you to ask yourself: How low is low? Lehman Brothers went to zero. That was the all time low for Lehman……Zero.

CHAPTER 4

PICKING STOCKS LIKE A PRO

We are now on step number three: How to choose a stock. I want to teach you how to choose a stock like a professional. The professionals say that eighty percent of your trading success is entries, but I think 80 percent of your trading success is choosing a proper tradeable stock. If you're trading Fannie Mae, I mean, like, come on! The stock doesn't move. You're not going to make any money, right? If it's a rubbish stock, you're not going to make money. I'm going to teach you how professionals choose stocks and how professionals find proper tradeable stocks, okay? Let's go on with our lesson.

There are many avenues for traders to use to pick a stock. Before get to that, let's find out

How Not to Pick a Stock

1. Have a friend recommend a stock.

2. Have a broker recommend a stock.

3. Have your dentist recommend a stock.

4. Subscribe to a newsletter that gives you top picks for the week.

5. Sit on your couch, drink a beer and watch "Guru Sam" on TV and pray that he or she will give you the next incredible stock picks.

You might be saying to yourself:

- Huh? I've been using my broker!
- I ask my friends, "Hey, what are you trading? Is it a good stock?"
- I subscribe to a newsletter online and enjoy paying $97 a month or $300 a month and they give me stock picks.

Please tell me, how's that working out for you?

Please, for the love of your financial security, no! Hogs and sheep rely on others to find stocks for them to trade. What happens in the end? Sheep and hogs get slaughtered. Maybe you are not a hog or a sheep per se, but if you're relying on a friend who just completed a one-day course or a two-day course, do you think she is completely sane? Maybe she is sane, but market sane? Come on, really? Are you kidding me right now? No! You can't rely on "Guru Sam".

We spoke about this. "Guru Sams" may be telling you to buy the stock because they're on the other side of the trade. If you rely on your broker, your broker is on the other side of the trade. Oh come on. No, no, no, no, no! The price of trading and investing is taking active responsibility in all parts of your trading-- not just sitting here and learning the information, not just depositing money into your trading account and definitely not just actively trading but finding stocks, right? Professionals don't rely on somebody else to find stocks to trade... well, let's talk about that.

It is true that professionals who work for institutions rely on people to find stocks for them. But let's face it, the people who are finding stocks for the professionals to trade have mathematics degrees from MIT.

They're Harvard grads and MIT and LSE (London School of Economics) graduates; they're using those people to find trading opportunities for them. Right? We don't have those kinds of people on our team people to find stocks for us.

However, there is a way that I'm going to teach you that will show you what the professionals are trading before the hogs and sheep discover them.

You cannot ask other sheep or hogs for stock recommendations. If you do, **you are on the way to the slaughter house just like them**! It's like the blind leading the blind. Are you going to ask a blind man if there's a car coming? Come on. Are you serious? Maybe they'll hear that the car is coming but he doesn't truly know. HE CAN'T SEE! It's just crazy! This is what we do as beginners! To be successful you must take active responsibility in your own stock choices.

You cannot ask your broker for stock picks because of the simple rule. The market is a zero sum game. If they are telling you to buy ABC stock, what side of the trade are they on? We spoke about this right? That is a question that you have to ask yourself: "What side of the trade are they on if they're telling me to buy the stock? Could it be they're on the other side of the trade?"

Let's refine our process of finding and choosing a stock.

Where do I find stocks if I cannot use all the channels that I've been using in the past? The most reliable source I've found and that other professional traders are using is Investor's Business Daily. Look, I'm not getting paid by Investor's Business Daily and I don't use the CAN SLIM method of trading. They have their own method of trading. I don't use that. But I digress ... especially regarding trading in stocks, I've found incredible trading opportunities on Investor's Business Daily.

One of the stocks that I found on Investor's Business Daily in 2007 was POT. I was looking through Investor's Business Daily on a Monday and I found POT. I was like: "Oh my gosh! Look at the stock and it's a $30 stock ." The price of POT was perfect for my trading account. As a beginner trader you don't want to start trading high flying, high priced stocks at the beginning of your career.

You want to stick to lower priced stocks. In the third book of this series, I'm going to go deeper into the art and science of finding tradeable and stable stocks suitable for beginner traders. I don't endorse penny stocks;

they are too volatile for my trading style. I've actually found that people who trade penny stocks are gamblers and not professional traders. **I'm sorry to say this, but penny stocks are too risky**.

Let's return back to my story of Investor's Business Daily.

POT was a very cheap stock and I looked at it and I thought: "Oh, this stock is stable, it's an emerging stock so not too many players yet and it's in the perfect price range for my trading account." I said, "Okay. I'm just going to try this Investor's Business Daily. If it works it works, if it doesn't, I'd cancel my subscription." Oh my gosh! I traded POT for 5 months. That stock went up from $39 to $75 ... in five months. I was astounded and thought: "I am convinced. I am an addict. I am sold on Investor's Business Daily." Stocks on IBD don't always work, but I have found more trading opportunities and quality stocks in Investor's Business Daily than I have found in Wall Street Journal or Barrons or any other source of finding stocks.

I love Investor's Business Daily. And let me reiterate that I'm not getting paid by them. I'm just telling you how to find proper stocks.

What should you look for in Investor's Business Daily?

First off, if you subscribe to Investor's Business Daily, you'll find that the Monday edition is the best. IBD's top 50 lists is the best part of the paper. IBD will give you stocks that are being accumulated by institutional traders. These are professional traders buying up these stocks. You want to be part of that action. You don't want to be buying stock if the professionals are not doing so.

There's also a section called Stocks on the Move on their website. These stocks are more suited for day and swing traders. Professionals are acquiring those stocks and you want to be on the side of the professionals. What Investor's Business Daily does is it looks at stocks that the banks and professionals and hedge funds and mutual funds are acquiring. If those stocks are being acquired by institutions, you know that there is an insane amount of money going into those stocks. Those stocks are going to rise. It doesn't always happen but more times than not, **the stocks suggested by IBD move**.

Sometimes it takes six months for it to happen. Sometimes it takes three months to happen. You know that institutions and the professionals, the big boys, with lots of money are acquiring the stock. You want to be in on those stocks. Be contrary to the professionals at your peril.

Let's review the other golden section: IBD Top 50 Stocks with charts. That section comes out on Monday like I mentioned earlier. IBD gives you 50 stocks that are being acquired by professionals and institutions and hedge funds and mutual funds, and then you can look at those stocks and pick which ones you would like to trade.

These are the two sections of IBD: Top 50 and Stocks on the Move. That's where I have found precious, beautiful stocks. It's just incredible trading opportunities.

Let's Do Our Homework

Get a two week free subscription on Investor's Business Daily. You just go to investors.com and then sign up for the two week free subscription. Browse through the Stocks on the Move section or IBD Top 50. Pick a stock that you might like to trade and start your research. Okay? Now, how are you going to start ... how are you going to go about your research? Go to Yahoo Finance and then type in the stock symbol and put your 200 day period moving average.

We talked about the 200 day moving average in the last chapter. We need to figure out whether the stock is bullish or bearish. You need to know where your 200 day moving average is on that stock, right?

Professional traders always have five to ten stocks in the trading basket. Pick five to ten stocks and do some research on them. You want to follow those stocks or even trade those stocks in your demo trading account. To be able to master trading, you want to know who the players are, what the players are doing and what the players' opinions are about a stock (you can see the opinions by the size of the candles on a chart) and then know whether the stock is in a bullish or bearish trend and then demo trade the stock to improve your skill level of picking the right stocks.

So there you have it: your foundation to trading success.

All it takes to be a winner is the discipline to follow these three simple steps to a winning trade. From here on out, if you wish to succeed... stop gambling... stop blaming anyone other than yourself... and begin relying on your own analysis driven by the 3 Steps.

To loosely paraphrase Sun Tzu, know yourself... Know your enemy and 100 battles are won before they are ever fought.

What does this have to do with trading? Everything.

If you know what the professional traders are doing this is like "following the cat to the rat". The professionals will clue you in on what sectors, commodities and companies to follow, what side "the smart money" is on in each trade and what trades are in play or on the move.

But, simply understanding what the professionals, the smart money, is trading and what side they are on is not enough. Who do you think looks after your own interests better than you? No one. As I shared with you earlier, this book is big on personal accountability and ownership of your decisions to be successful. You have to CONFIRM the theories you gather from analyzing the professionals' trading. Is the market trending up or down? The professionals are not right ALL of the time and you shouldn't be willing to risk your own capital based entirely on someone else's analysis.

- So if the market is trending up and the professionals are buying, you buy.
- If the market is going down and the professionals are selling, you short.
- If there is any disagreement between the professionals' side of the trade and the market trend, you wait.

As a recap, all you have to do to be an overall winning trader is to stick to the 3 Steps. But, you aren't going to make a dime simply reading a book. You have to get out there and trade! But some of you my friends may be a bit hesitant because you may have been burned. If this is you, if you have any hesitancy whatsoever, do not rush to E-trade just yet. I want you to turn the page to Chapter 5 and learn why beginners generally always lose everything. It's time to give you a coat of armor before you do battle with your three weapons: **The 3 Steps.**

PART 3

PREVENT BEGINNER'S BAD LUCK

CHAPTER 5

WHY DO BEGINNERS HAVE CRAPPY RETURNS?

1. They lack education

2. They lack a mentor who will help them advance through the learning curve

3. They have a gambler's mentality

4. They approach the stock market with LOTS OF FEAR

5. They fail to plan every single trade

THEY LACK TRADING EDUCATION

I've heard it all; I've heard all the excuses under the sun about why beginner traders don't want to invest in their education. Here are a few of them.

I've heard it all; I've heard all the excuses under the sun about why beginner traders don't want to invest in their education. Here are a few of them.

1. " Let me make some money first, then I'll take a trading class"

This is by far the most dangerous excuse I've ever heard. We just reviewed ad nauseum as to why beginners lose everything. A person giving this excuse will take their trading stake into the market and lose it due to inexperience, lack of discipline and panic. They'll then blame the "rigged" Wall Street casino and miss out on the consistent profits that could have been made had they had the foresight to invest in their education before investing in the stock market.

2. "I don't have the money to take a class"

But you have the money to trade? This is almost worse than excuse numero uno. This is like saying, " I can pay cash for a house... But I can't afford the homeowner's insurance." Do you think it is really wise to leave such an important asset to your family unprotected? It is FAR less expensive to learn inside a community like Stock Market For Beginners School than it is to learn from experience by REPEATEDLY losing your shirt.

3. "I can read a few books, which should be enough to get me started."

Yup, just enough to be dangerous... to your trading account. Would you entrust your savings to a "professional" who "took a few courses on finance in community college"? Of course not. Hold yourself to a higher educational standard and prepare properly for your future as a stock market investor.

4. "I'm a slow learner; it's going to take me a long time to master stock market content."

Then why are you in a rush to go trade the stock market? Until you've mastered the material you have three options:

Leave your money in a checking account and let it be eaten away by inflation; leave your money to a professional who will pay himself rather large commissions for marginal performance... Or join a stock market trading community and take matters into your own CAPABLE hands.

5. "My spouse will not let me."

This is a valid excuse. "A happy wife (or husband) is a happy life". But remember my lovely couple in Florida? Could they have been happier and more financially secure if the husband or wife had known how to look after and grow all the money they worked so hard for?

6. "I can watch YouTube videos to get some trading ideas."

This is NOT a valid excuse. I know you might be thinking that this is not an excuse. You might be thinking, "Hey Thembi, I don't have the money to invest in trading education yet." Ok, that might be valid, but this is what I know. Professional traders who spend their time trading the stock market and teaching their trading system are not going to give you their trading strategies for FREE. They will teach you the WHAT, the WHY and a little bit of the HOW, never the exact how.

It's not that they are bad people; it's just that teaching the exact how takes more than a 15 minute time slot. When I teach the exact how, it takes me 90-120 minutes to make sure that a beginner trader understands the concept. The exact how cannot be taught in a 5-15 minute video.

BEGINNERS LACK A MENTOR WHO WILL HELP THEM ADVANCE THROUGH THE LEARNING CURVE.

"YOU CAN'T GIVE YOURSELF A PROFESSIONAL HAIR CUT".

I used to think that I could master everything on my own. I took a short Forex trading course when I was 20. After the trading course, I quit my day job and started trading the Forex market full time. I think it was pure luck that I traded that long without wiping out my trading account. It took me four years to build a huge trading account. The downside is that it took me only 2 weeks to completely destroy the same trading account.

It was not until I started working for a trading firm in New York City that I learned the value of having a mentor. I learned that a mentor helps you learn and implement the education and trading system faster than you can on your own. I learned that a good mentor or coach holds you accountable to your trading plan. And the most valuable lesson I learned, is that a good trading coach sees your blind spots better than you can see them.

Trading can sometime be very challenging, some days you're up, some weeks and even months you're winning, and then you hit the trader's slump. A good mentor and coach will help you stay positively focused on your goals and your financial future when the going gets tough and you want to quit.

Chapter 6

Know When To Hold 'Em and When to Fold 'Em

They have a gambler's mentality

There is an art and a science to trading the stock market that anyone can learn. There are rules and laws that if broken will erode your trading capital quicker than going to Vegas for a quick weekend gambling trip.

I once had a student who insisted on investing in gold stocks because she had heard that gold was a stable commodity to invest in. Let me tell you that EVERYTHING is safe to invest in when you know what you are doing. She was buying gold stocks left and right, with no plan of taking her profits once the stocks had moved up. As her stock market mentor, I had to warn her that what she was doing was not trading; instead she was exhibiting the signs of a gambler.

After sometime I realized that I had to let her go as a client because I knew that I couldn't teach her how to trade like a professional trader. She was set in her investing ways and I was not the right mentor for her. Three months later she had found another mentor who encouraged her to keep buying gold stocks while advising her that she was on the right track. I knew that this was dangerous. However, I know when it is time to mind my own business. Her style of investing was dangerous because she didn't know when she was going to sell the gold stocks for a profit. She didn't have a plan. She was just hoping that her gold stocks would keep rising until she became the next Warren Buffet.

Sadly, two months ago, she sent me an email after she got badly burned in her gold stocks and had lost all her profits and some of her initial investment. Remember our case study in GLD a few chapters back? Go back and look at the chart of GLD so that you can understand that I'm not making this stuff up. In fact, type GLD into Yahoo Finance and add the 200 Day Moving Average to a candlestick chart. You'll see she might as well have thrown her money into a fire! Failure due to negligence, ignorance and greed happens. My intention is that it doesn't happen to you.

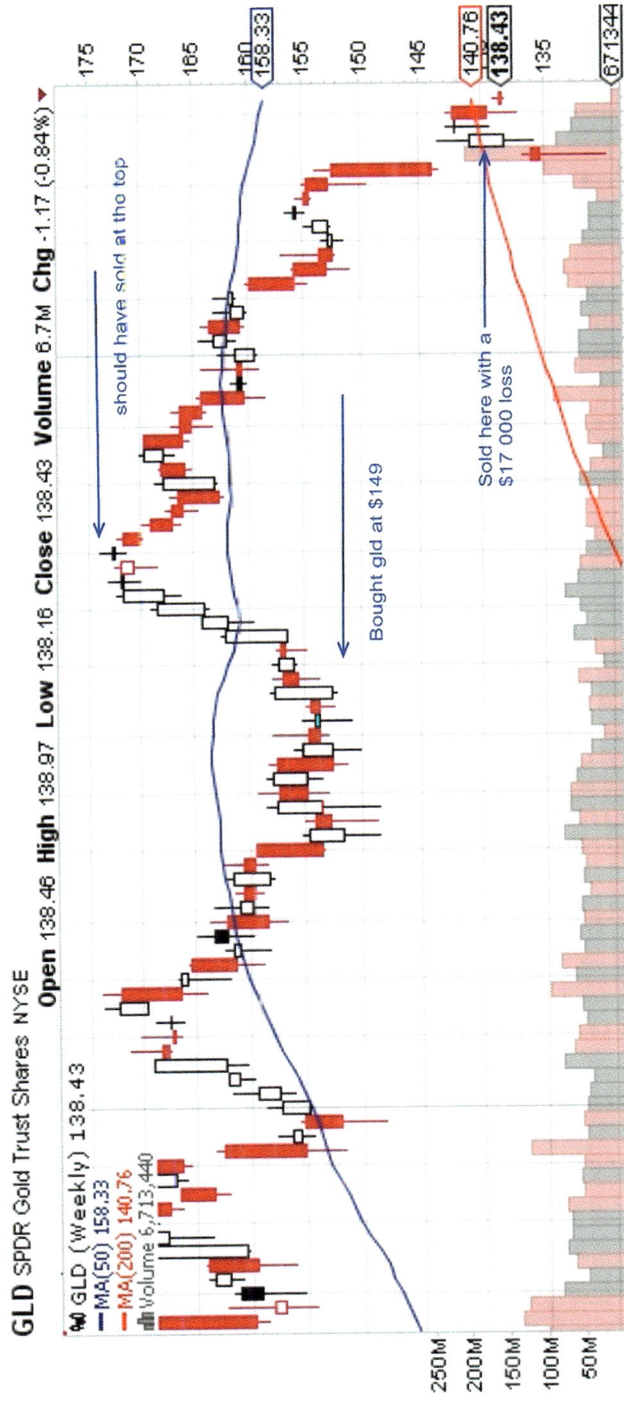
GLD SPDR Gold Trust Shares NYSE
Open 138.46 High 138.97 Low 138.16 Close 138.43 Volume 6.7M Chg -1.17 (-0.84%)
GLD (Weekly) 138.43
MA(50) 158.33
MA(200) 140.76
Volume 6,713,440
should have sold at the top
Bought gld at $149
Sold here with a
$17 000 loss

Here is the rundown of the trade: she bought 500 shares of GLD at $149. She didn't take profits when GLD reached $173, at the peak. Instead she held the shares as the price went lower and finally sold at a loss at $139. She lost $5000 in 7 months. At the beginning of the trade she was positive. She actually had made over $11,000, but she didn't sell her shares, she was gambling, she wanted more profits and in the end the gambling mentality cost her $11 000 in profits **and $5000.00 in losses.**

I feel sad when beginner traders lose money in the stock market, especially when they had positive trades. Imagine what she could have done with all that money. She could have reinvested it into another surefire stock and kept earning $5-10,000 every 5 months. Those kinds of returns are better than any 401k or IRA can produce.

I urge you to have a plan. Know when you are going to take profits. The stock market is not a Vegas casino. You have to take profits when you make them to avoid disasters like this.

CHAPTER 7
THE STOCK MARKET BOOGIE MAN

THEY APPROACH THE STOCK MARKET WITH LOTS OF FEAR

I hope that I have not amped up the fear of loss for you. Instead, I hope that the story I shared with you about my client and her GLD fiasco will inspire you to take precaution when trading your hard earned money. I would rather you have a healthy dose of fear instead of carelessly thinking that you are invincible and will never make dumb mistakes in the market. When you know that you can lose your money, you will be more willing to implement the 3 Steps to building wealth in the stock market.

With that said, traders who approach the market with fear, or with paralyzing terror, usually never achieve greatness. Any small movement in the stock that they are trading scares the living lights out of them and they take profits prematurely. I want you to understand that stocks move up and down on a daily basis. It is normal to watch your stock go down a little and then find its support and then start moving back up again. Traders and investors who have not learned how to understand the movement of candles and how particular stocks move get spooked out of their winners and then end up chasing stocks higher and lose money.

The common mindset on Wall Street is that traders have to be like a robot and have no emotions when they are trading. I think this is a whole lot of garbage. We are human beings first, and then traders.

We are going to feel fear and excitement in every single trade. **The million dollar question is: are you going to allow yourself to be ruled by fear every time to enter a trade?**

When you have comprehensive step-by-step education, you will experience a small amount of fear. However, you'll be able to act and trade in spite of your fears. You'll have a solid foundation that fear cannot break.

My advice to you is that instead of fearing the stock market, respect the stock market and know that it is always right. Your job as a trader is to listen to what it is telling you to do and just follow along with it. "The trend is your friend". The stock market uses candles to communicate with traders. It's our job as investors and traders to learn the language of the stock market and follow the instructions that the stock market is giving us.

Below is an example of how the stock market communicates through candles. As you'll see, I've circled a candle. That candle is called a doji. The doji is a stock market sign letting you know that money is flowing out of a stock and it's time for you to take profits. Look at what happened after that doji: The price of the stock tumbled.

If you ignore the signs the stock market gives to you, you end up losing money. So, as you can see, you don't need to fear the stock market, with the correct education you can tell what the stock market is about to do just by reading candles. Here is one of my earliest trades as a beginner which cost me quite a bit of money and taught me a lesson that I'll NEVER FORGET:

BIDU Baidu, Inc. Nasdaq GM
Open 97.04 High 97.38 Low 95.50 Close 96.35 Volume 3.1M Chg -0.29 (-0.30%)
BIDU (Weekly) 96.35
MA(50) 103.00
MA(200) 100.48
Volume 3,066,151
Should have sold once I saw the reversal signal
Stock carried on going lower
60M
40M
20M

CHAPTER 8
FAIL TO PLAN... PLAN TO FAIL

THEY FAIL TO PLAN EVERY SINGLE TRADE

This is one of the biggest mistakes beginner traders make in the stock market. They fail to plan. When you fail to plan your trades, you end up holding stocks way past their expiration date. You have to know what price you will enter your stock and what price you are willing to take profits.

If you treat investing like a small business, you will create a business plan--or what we call a trading plan. A trading plan helps you create rules that will help you succeed. A trading plan helps you avoid staying in a trade way past its expiration date. A trading plan allows you to stay focused and helps you avoid gambling.

If you create a trading plan and it doesn't have all of the 3 Steps to building stock market wealth, you have a flawed trading plan. It's not only important to have a trading plan, but it is vitally important to have a trading plan that prevents you from breaking or deviating from the 3 Steps to Build Stock Market Wealth.

CONCLUSION - GET TO WORK... MAKE SOME MONEY

Please understand, my goal is to teach you "how to fish" rather than just give you a fish. I want to give you the ability to "feed" your dreams, your retirement and your financial well being. I've shown you the most vital concept to your trading success: 3 Steps to Build Stock Market Wealth as a winning professional level trader.

I would love for you to use this kindle book as a guide for knowing and understanding who the professionals are and what they are doing, identifying market trends and identifying the stocks on the move.

In fact, Yahoo will assist you with Step 2 and Investor's Business Daily will provide Step 3. You just need to do your homework to knock out Step 1 and then "pull the trigger" on the trading opportunities you found.

But you still need a plan and I highly encourage you to find a mentor to teach, coach, support and guide you through the beginning of your "professional class" trading career. I personally can't think of a single world class athlete, doctor, attorney, politician or entrepreneur who didn't or doesn't have a mentor. That's something to definitely ponder regarding mentorship and trading the stock market.

All that aside, if you are looking for assistance in the creation of your plans and want detailed information regarding the secret weapon to the 3 Step Plan: Technical Analysis, I very much want you to visit and explore my educational website for beginning traders just like you at: Stock Market For Beginner School

Now, if you are highly motivated and very serious about reaching the professional level in your trading and agree with me a mentor is the single best trading education investment you will find and you promise:

- To swear off those snake oil trading seminars that farm Hogs for slaughter in the market.

- To stop using your friends, your relatives, your broker, TV programs on CNBC or Bloomberg and all the "gurus" out there who lead the Sheep to the slaughter in the market.

I would be honored and delighted to be your mentor and:

- Hold you accountable to your Trading Strategies

- Coach and Guide you as you formulate your Trading Strategies

- Teach you the detailed ins and outs of The 3 Step Plan

- Teach you professional Technical Analysis so you know when to buy and sell

- Keep you focused and positive during those few losing decisions

- Keep you balanced when you're smashing the market with your trades

I've already taught you how to identify the *right* trading opportunities. Now is the time to learn how to execute them.

Contact Information

Thembi and Busi Buthelezi are the founders of Stock Market For Beginners School, a company devoted to teaching beginner investors and traders around the world how to consistently make up to 30-50% profits in the stock market, experience fewer loses, create a solid foundation for financial independence through stock market investing and building the confidence and self assurance to manage their own money.

Thembi and Busi created The Stock Market For Beginners System, the proven step-by-step, paint by numbers program that shows beginner investors exactly how to spot buying opportunities, find winning stocks and consistently make money in the stock market, in record time. Through their courses, coaching programs, and products, Thembi and Busi show their students how to replace their 9-5 job income, build wealth, create financial independence and never rely on a stock broker for stock tips.

As two of the most influential and heart centered Wall Street Traders and investing mindset mentors, the sisters' down-to-earth yet powerful presentations have become renowned. They are sought-after and much-loved educators and mentors to hundreds of heart-centered, thrill seeking investors and traders around the globe.

Highlights from Thembi's inspiring career include: 12 years in the financial markets. 5 years spent as an independent currency (Forex) trader. 6 years spent trading the equities market first for a trading fund, then independently branching off on her own.

Highlights from Busi's inspiring career include: 6 years as an independent Forex trader. After working as a programmer, Busi decided that trading the Forex market was far more exciting than writing code for a living. Busi now writes code for the love of staying current with the different programming languages, but her first love is trading the Forex market and developing beginner traders.

Thembi and Busi have consistently and repeatedly mentored beginner traders and investors on how to take advantage of bullish and bearish markets. Through their process they have helped absolute beginner traders achieve 80% accuracy in the market. Creating the most repeatable and actionable Stock Market For Beginners System for beginner investors and traders.

Inquiries: http://stockmarketforbeginnersschool.com/contact-us/

Password needed to access your free audio of the book

Go to: http://www.stock-market-for-beginners-school.com/

Password: ilovestocks

27966708R00045

Made in the USA
Lexington, KY
01 December 2013